If I Could Change The Weather

by Angela Miles

With love for my three little inspirations, Miles, Gabriel and Ethan
and with special thanks to my husband, Bradford King, the love of my life
Copyright 1999 Angela King, Photographs Copyright Associated Press Wide World Photos
Published by Painted Bridge Publishing, Post Office Box 1286, Ashland, VA 23005, www.paintedbridge.com
Design by Apple Pie Graphics (804) 644-2033, Printed by Choice Communications, Inc. (800) 255-0300

If I could change the weather, there would be bread for a little Rwandan girl. I would rain warm bread and butter, scatter gentle showers of rice, and leave puddles of pudding. I would send a rain of food upon Rwanda and upon all the lands where people are hungry and long for anything at all to eat.

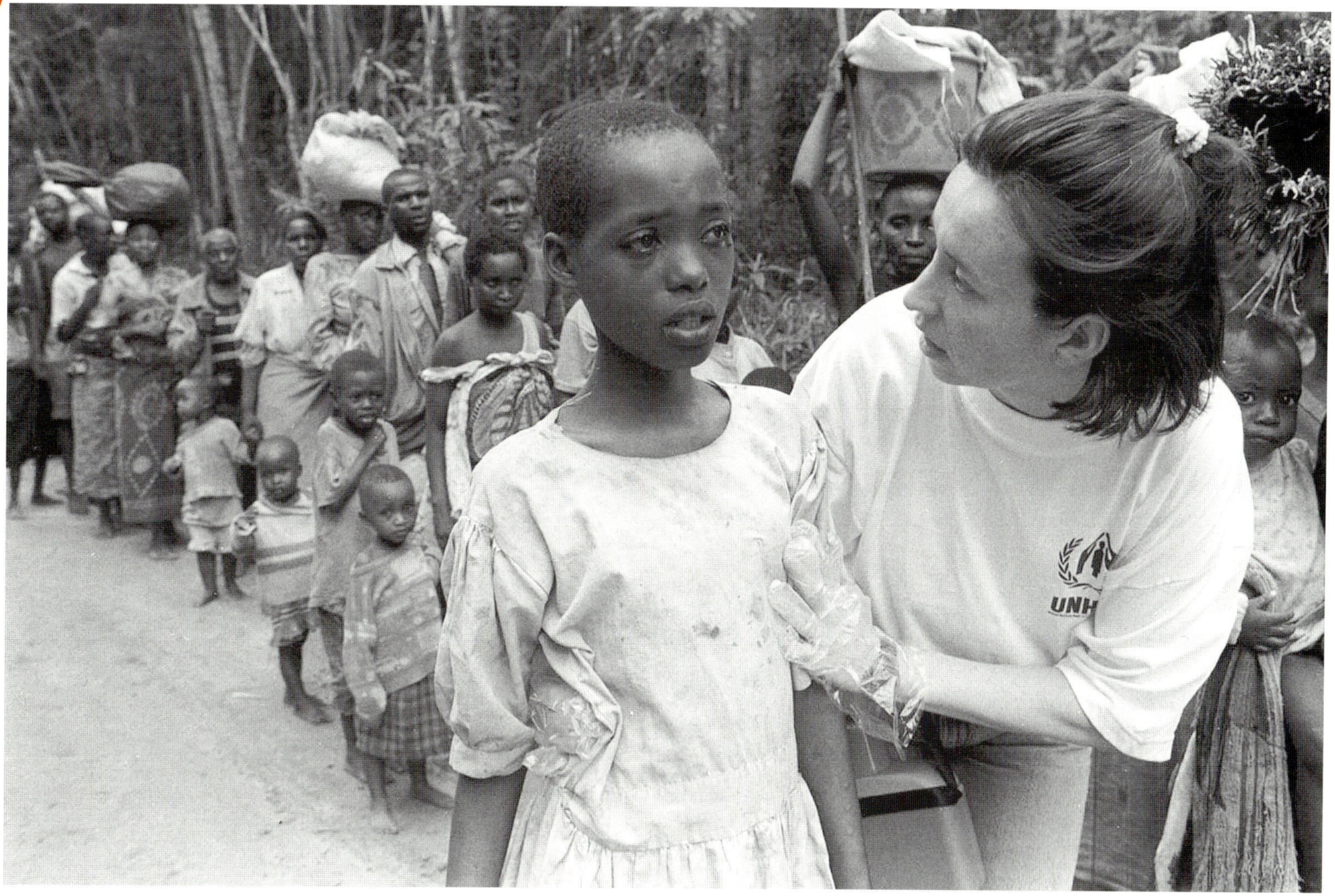

If I could change the weather, there would be peace in the homes of little Bosnian children. I would blanket Bosnia and every angry nation in mounds of soothing snow. Each flake would float like a tiny angel, descending with grace to the ground below. As softly as a sigh, the cascading crystals of icy white would cool the tempers of those who would rather fight than forgive.

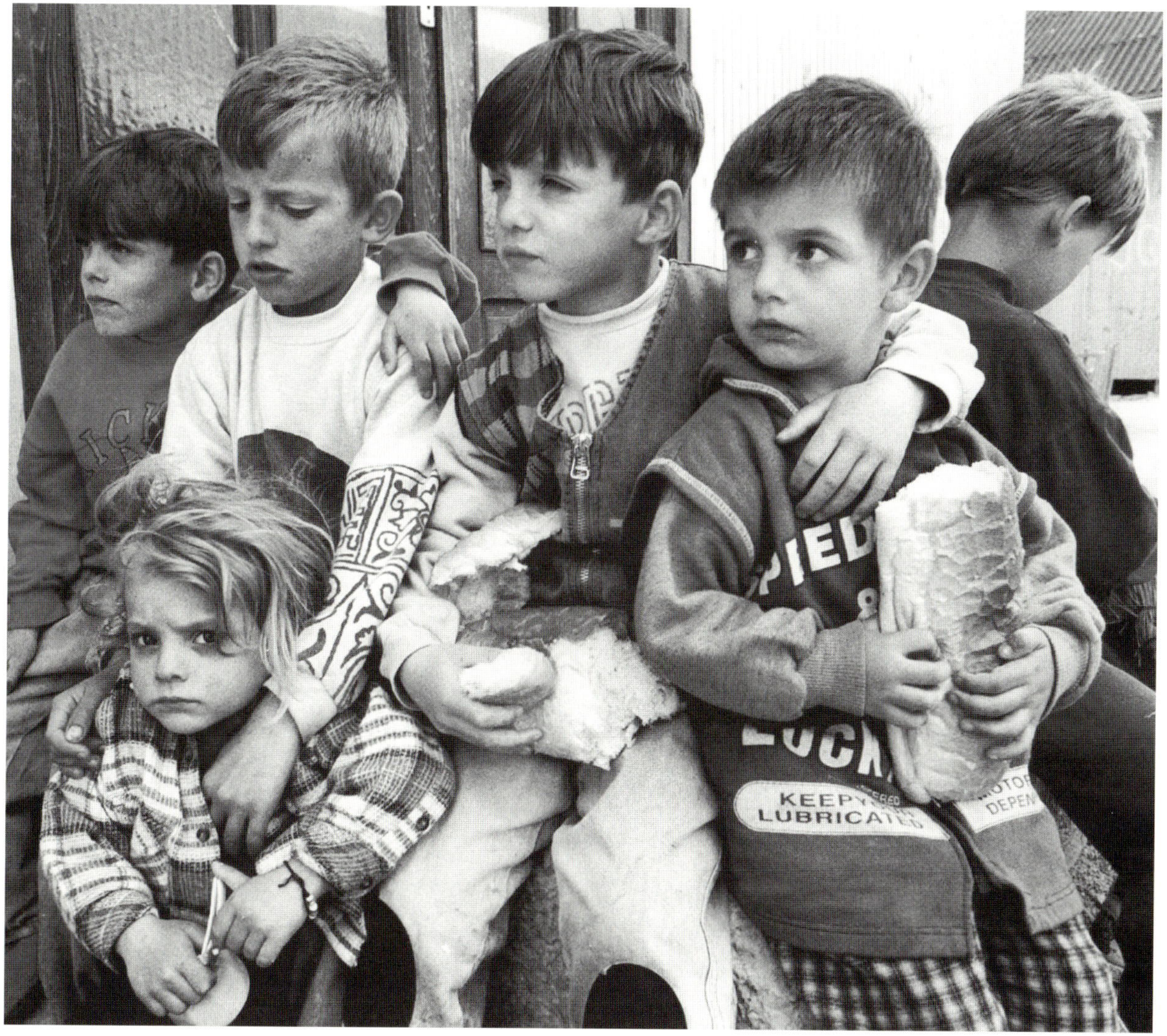

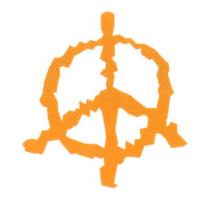

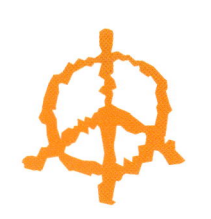

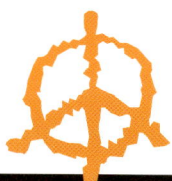

If I could change the weather, a little Russian boy would have bright hope for a family to love him and a future as wonderful as his dreams. I would send great winds of change for Russia and for every country struggling to make progress. I would send gales of good will to end the bitterness and sorrow of so many years.

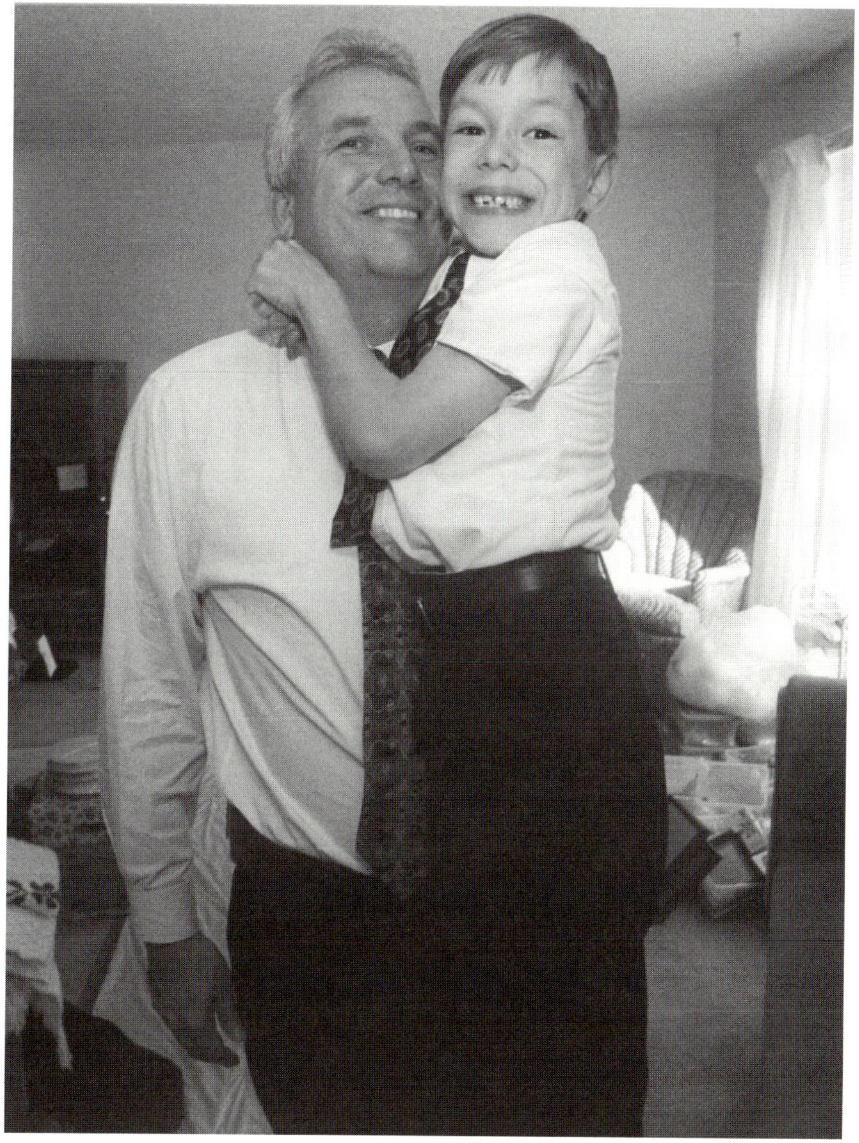

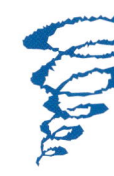

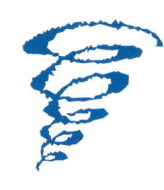

If I could change the weather, a little baby in America would have a warm place to rest. I would offer a lush summer breeze so no child would ever have to sleep in the cold. It would bring homes and heat for those who now go without. It would end all despair and dry every tear of longing.

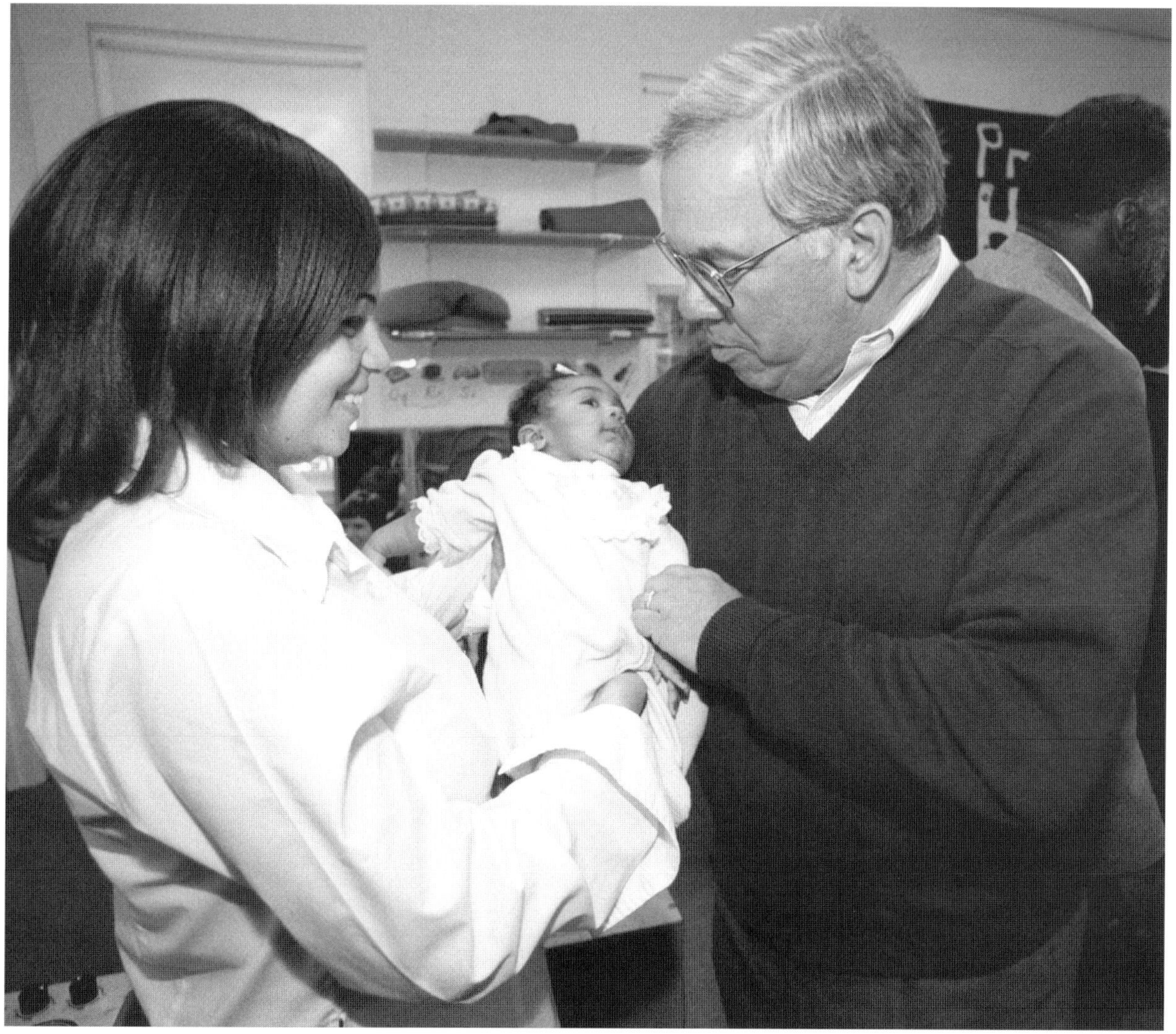

If I could change the weather, no little boy or little girl would have to feel afraid. I would surround them with the fierce force of a tornado. I would help them know that even in the worst of times, God lives in their hearts and that in the center of a storm we are always protected.

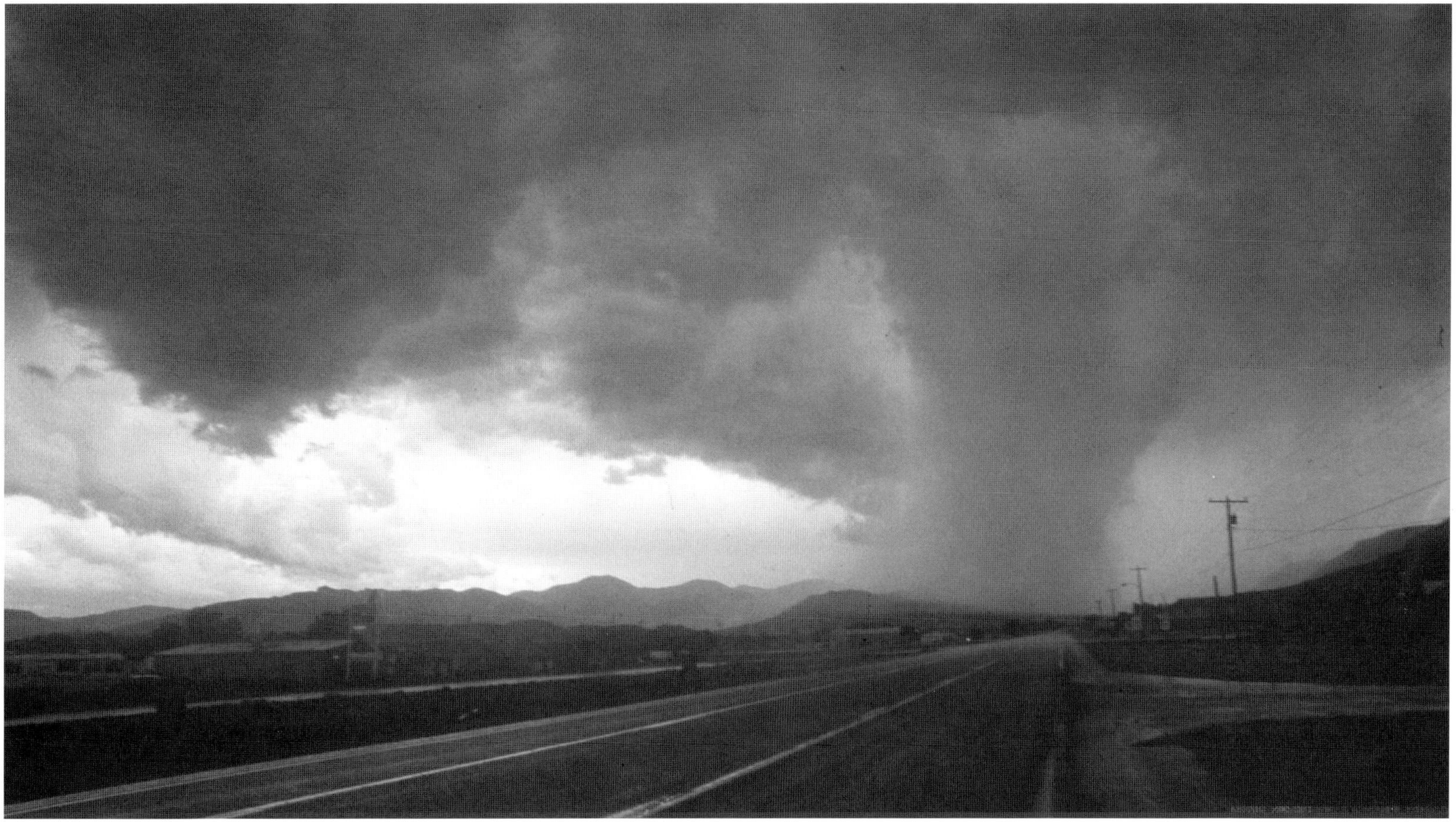

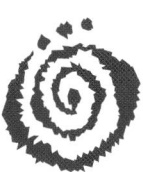

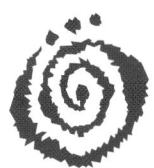

If I could change the weather, children who struggle through sickness would suddenly feel healthy and strong. I would use the glow of a smiling sun to cast beams of love and healing on everyone.

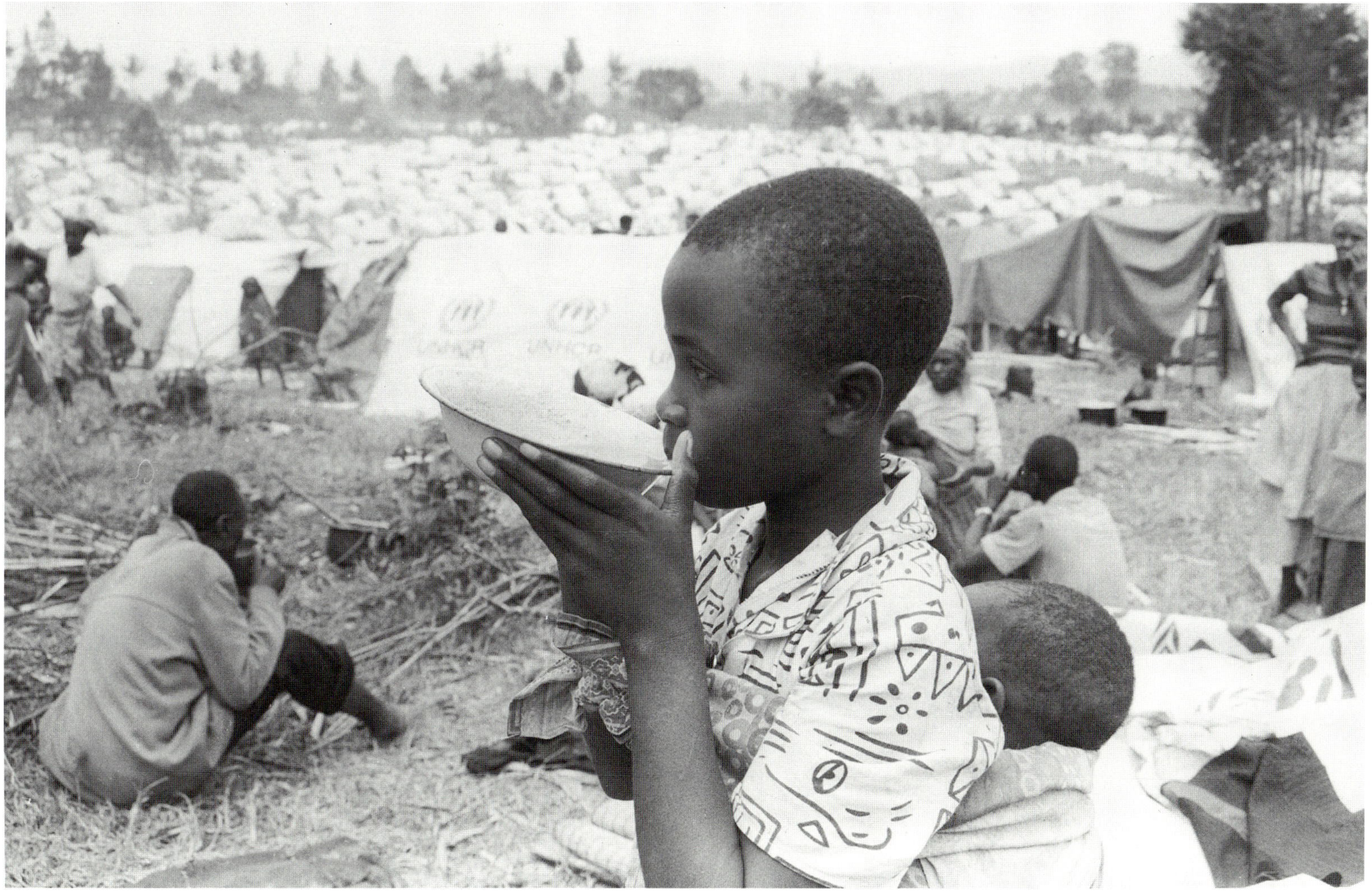
UNHCR
UNHCR

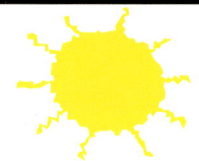

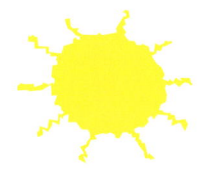

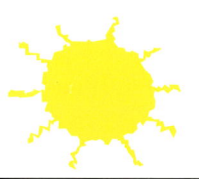

If I could change the weather, I would use it to chase away every illness, every sorrow, every hurt and fear.

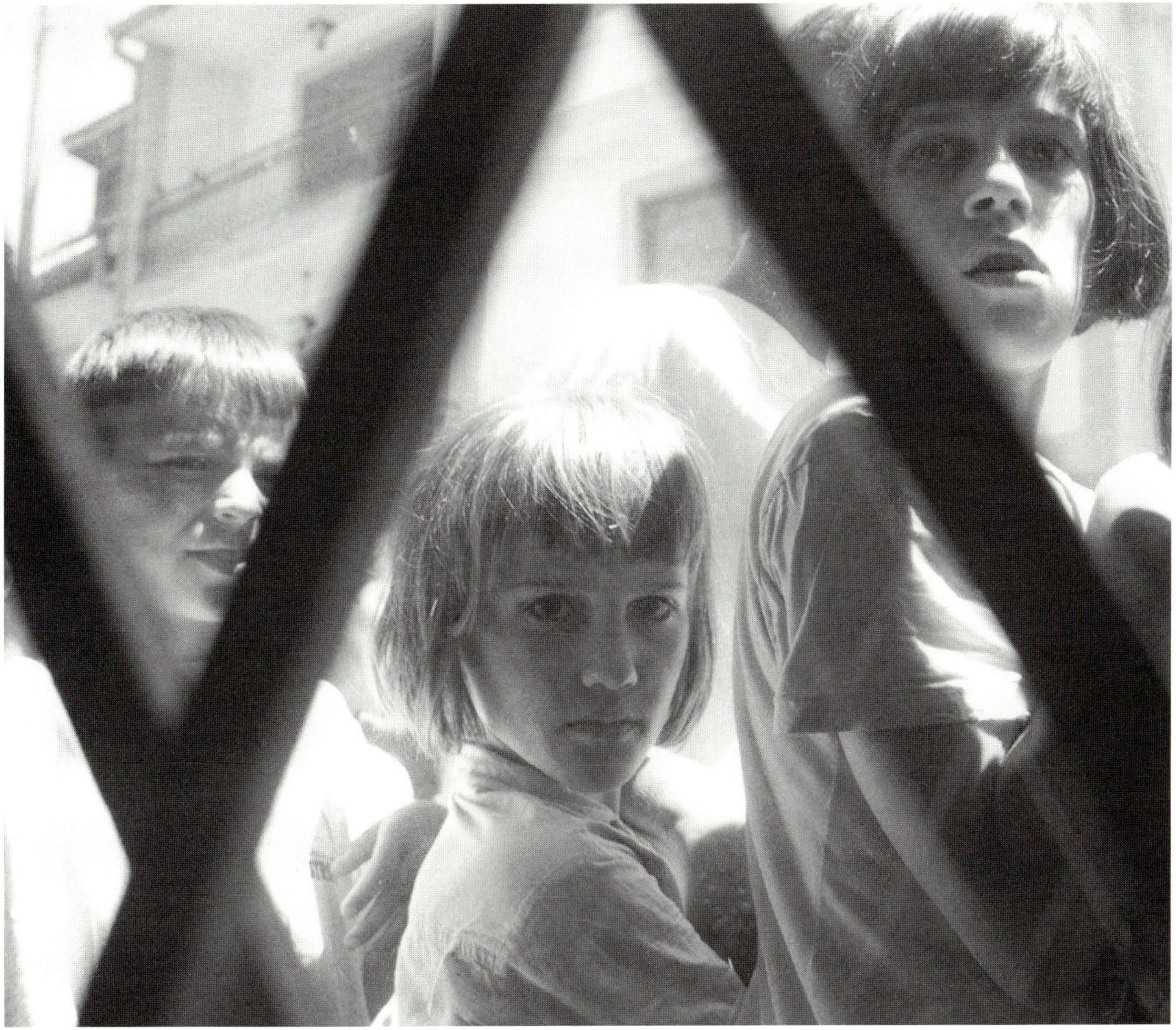

But I cannot change the weather. So instead I will trust the only One who can. I will trust that God knows the reason why people hurt and why people fight and why people are hungry in this world, even though I cannot understand. I will trust that God knows what is in the heart of every child, just as God knows what is in my heart, even if I have not told Him. I will trust that God is working out every problem in His own wise way and in His own perfect time.

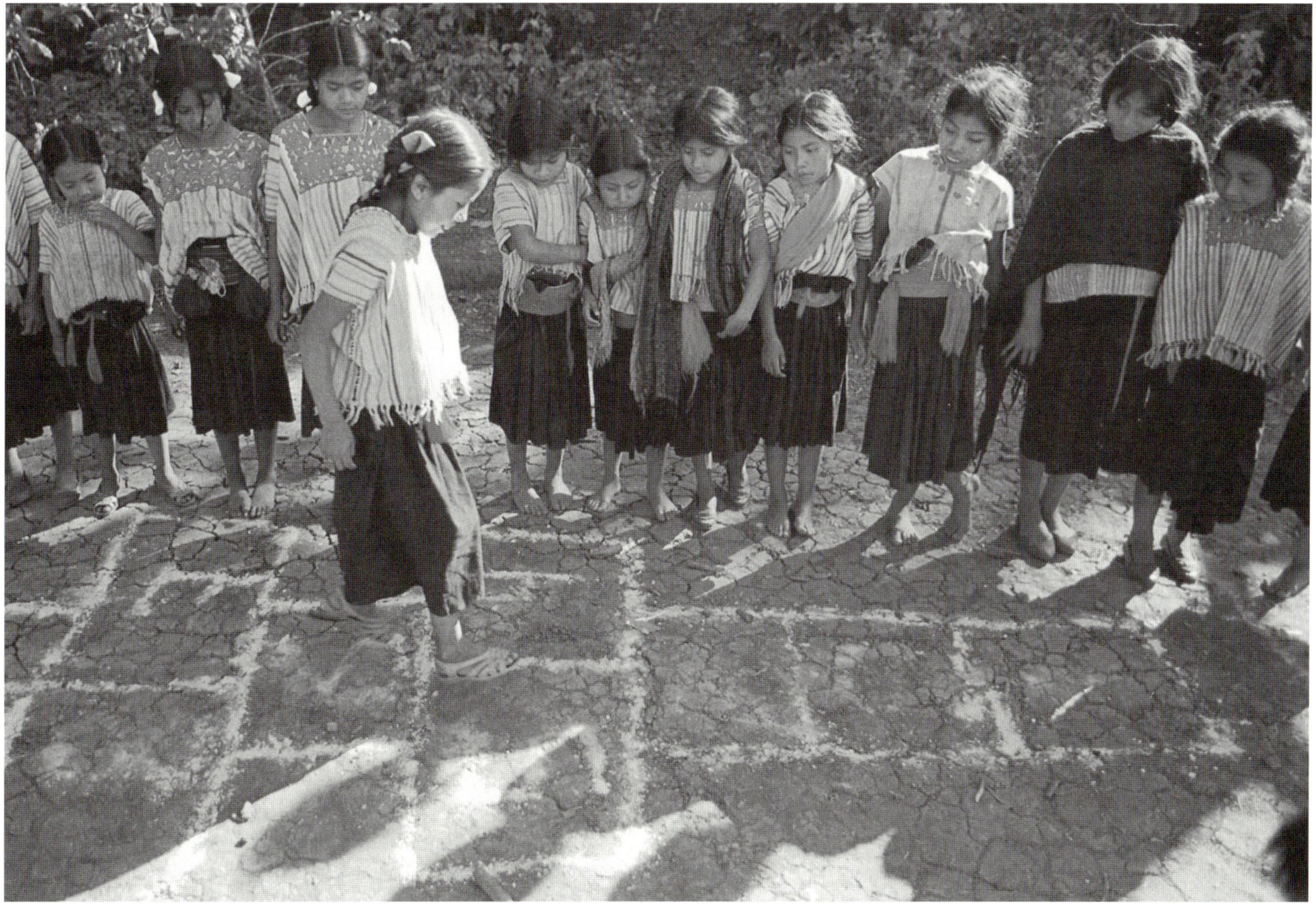

I cannot change the weather, but I can love with all my heart. I can ask God to watch over all the little children. I can tell Him that I care what happens to them. I can ask Him to tell me what more I can do to show my love. Only God can change the weather. Only God can send snow and wind and sun and rain. And only God can make rainbows after the storm. I cannot do any of these things on my own, but maybe God will let me help.

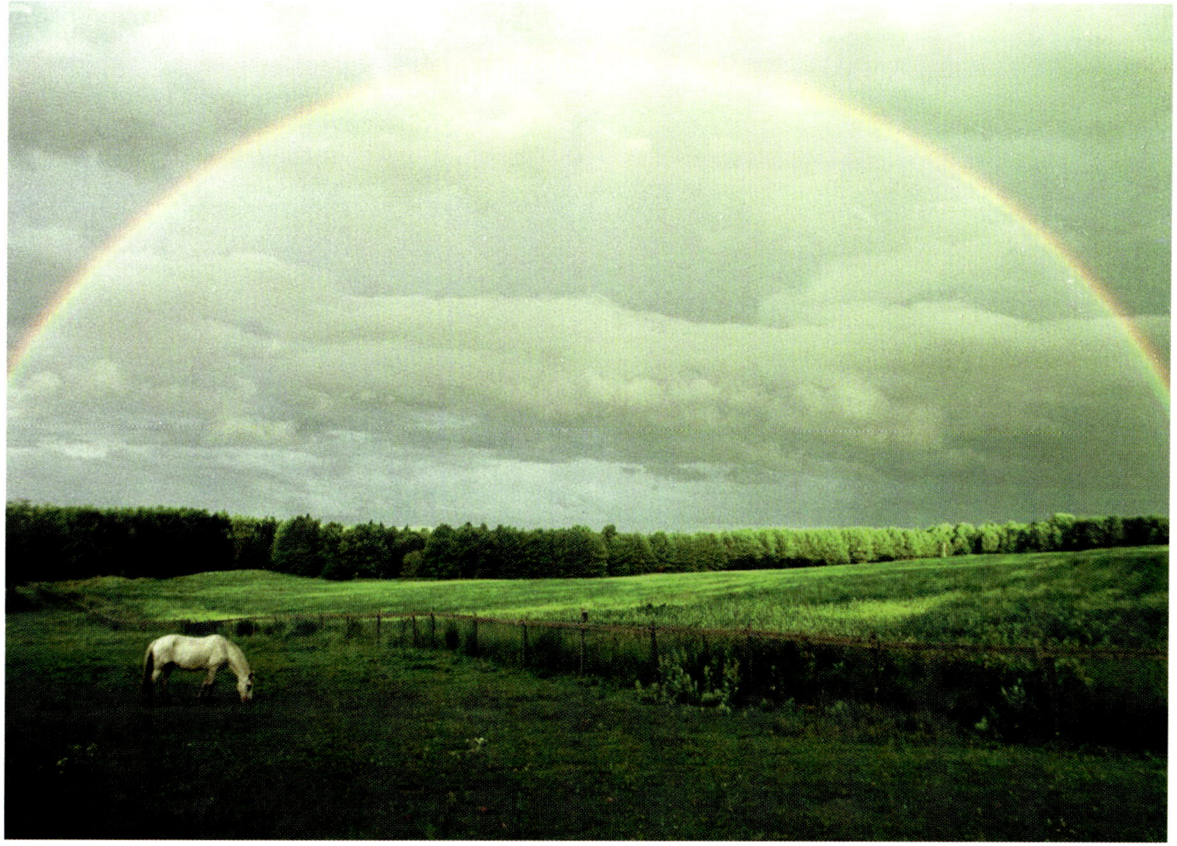

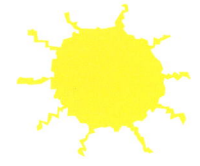

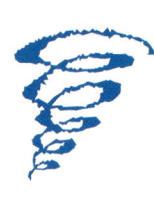

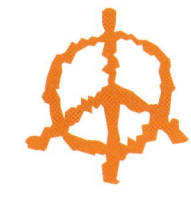

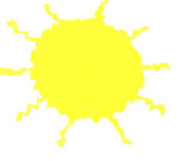

This book is dedicated to the continued service of Rainbow Kids, an organization that offers support and love for children and families affected by AIDS. If you would like to find out more about Rainbow Kids or offer donations of time or talent, you can contact them directly:

Rainbow Kids
Post Office Box 70844
Richmond, VA 23255

(804) 282-3538

If you would like to make a monetary donation, you may submit a check or money order to the following address:

Rainbow Kids Fund
First Virginia Bank-Colonial
Post Office Box 25279
Richmond, VA 23260